Ready, Set ...
WAIT!

By Patti R. Zelch

Illustrated by Connie McLennan

Far out over the warm ocean waters, clusters of storms join together; lightning lashes—thunder thumps. The wind grows stronger and begins to spin the clouds into a tight curl. A hurricane is brewing!

People gather powdered milk, beans, and other items, enough food and water for three days.

Fathers flicker flashlights on and off. Batteries are tested, radios tried, and shutters snapped shut.

Mothers drag plastic jugs from dark cabinet corners. "Fill each one with fresh water; we've no time to waste."

A young boy stops and stares at a squirrel scampering up a tree. The boy wonders—what do wild animals do before and during a hurricane?

On a reef below the water's surface, fish band together in large schools. They bolt this way and that, back and forth, twisting and turning—searching for food to fill their stomachs and for shelter in the deep grooves and caves of the coral. They know!

Dolphin pods squeeze closer—whistling and buzzing at one another. Their silver bodies streak through the waves heading for the safety of the open sea. They know!

Sharks explode from the shallows of a nearby bay. Instinctively, they head for the safety of the deep blue water. They know!

Lobsters crawl along the ocean floor. Their antennae twitch as they seek the safety of holes hidden in the sand. They know!

Offshore, manatees settle near
seagrass beds where they'll have
plenty to eat. Slowly, they sink to the
bottom and wait.

Up and down the coast, birds gather in flocks. "*Kwa, kwa*," calls a noisy seagull as it soars inland. Herons and pelicans glide toward the mangrove islands. They huddle there among the twisted roots. Waiting!

Crocodiles may crawl to open water or into deep canals and rivers that criss-cross the land. Concealed below the water's surface—they wait!

High above, dots of color sprinkle the sky. Butterflies dip down low, then flutter upward searching for shelter. Some wedge under rocks; others hide in hollow trees. They know!

Farther inland, rabbits race across the land looking for their burrows. Mice scurry through the grass toward higher ground. They know!

Dark clouds roll across the ocean. Sheets of rain fall. The wind howls, bending trees toward the ground. The hurricane is here!

For Creative Minds

Natural Disasters—What is a Hurricane?

Air pressure is the weight of the column of air that extends from the ground (or sea level) to the top of the atmosphere. It is measured in inches of mercury and is also called barometric pressure. The average air/barometric pressure at sea level is 29.92 inches. The lower the air pressure, the stronger the hurricane is.

storm surge

Storm surge is when the strong wind pushes ocean water onto land—much higher than the average high tide line.

average high tide line

average low tide line

These powerful storms develop over warm, tropical waters. The wind, storm surge, and heavy amounts of rain and lightening can cause a tremendous amount of damage. Because the storms need warm water, they begin to lose strength when they hit land.

Eye: The center of the storm around which the winds rotate. It is generally calm with no rain. The average width of an eye is 20 miles (32 km) across.

Hurricanes can be hundreds of miles/kilometers across.

The strong winds rotate

counterclockwise in the northern hemisphere

and clockwise in the southern hemisphere.

Eyewall: A band of thunder clouds around the eye. It has the most rain and the strongest winds of the storm.

What's in a Name? and Where in the World?

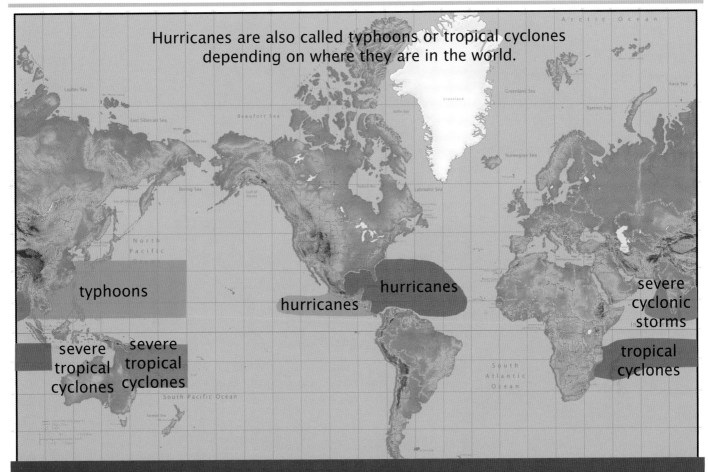

Hurricanes are also called typhoons or tropical cyclones depending on where they are in the world.

typhoons

hurricanes

hurricanes

severe cyclonic storms

severe tropical cyclones

severe tropical cyclones

tropical cyclones

Hurricanes: Season runs from June 1 to November 30 with the peak in September.

Hurricanes: Season runs late May/early June to late October/early November with the peak in late August/early September.

Severe cyclonic storms: There are two seasons a year: April to June with a peak in May, and again from late September to early December with a peak in November.

Severe tropical cyclones: Season runs from June 1 to November 30 with the peak in September.

Tropical cyclones: Season runs from late October/early November to May with two peaks: one in mid-January and the second in mid-February.

Severe tropical cyclones: Season runs from late October/early November to early May with a peak in late February/early March.

Typhoons: Can happen at any time of year, but most happen between July and November with a peak in late August/early September.

What's in a Number? and What Can the Storm Do?

Hurricanes and tropical storms cause all kinds of damage. The stronger the winds and the bigger the storm, the more damage they cause.

On land, winds can blow down trees, rip out windows, or tear roofs off buildings. High winds can even knock down poorly constructed buildings.

The storm surge can carry cars, boats, or even buildings inland. Areas that have shallow coastlines are more affected by storm surge than coasts with high bluffs or cliffs.

While the storm surge can cause flooding, so can the heavy rains. Hurricanes can dump 5 to 10 inches or more of rain in one day! Sometimes there is flooding hundreds of miles from the coast.

Buildings and people are not the only things affected by these storms. Wild animals can be affected, too. The strong waves can destroy coral reefs, which are homes to many animals. Storm surge carries salt water onto land and might kill some animals that can only live with fresh water. Pollution and debris from destroyed buildings can be carried out into the ocean where it can poison or hurt animals.

Fortunately, scientists who study the weather (meteorologists) can see when these storms begin to develop. They can project approximately how strong a storm is coming and can give us an approximation of where it will make landfall. While we can't stop a hurricane from coming ashore, we can prepare for it and then leave (evacuate) the area if we must. Like the animals in this book, we can prepare and wait.

Stages	Saffir-Simpson Hurricane Scale: Sustained Winds per Hour			Air Pressure	
	miles	knots	KM	millibar	inches
Tropical Depression	<38	<33	<62		
Tropical Storm	39-73	34-63	63-118		
Hurricane Level 1- minimal	74-95	64-82	119-153	>980	>28.94
Hurricane Level 2- moderate	96-110	83-95	154-177	979-965	28.91-28.50
Hurricane Level 3- extensive	111-130	96-113	178-209	964-945	28.47-27.91
Hurricane Level 4- extreme	131-155	114-135	210-249	944-920	27.88-27.17
Hurricane Level 5- catastrophic	>155	>135	>249	<920	<27.17

Preparing for the Storm

Watching the news and listening to the radio will give you an idea on where the storm might be heading. Once it looks like the storm is coming your way, you should start making preparations. Don't wait until it is too late.

A **hurricane watch** means that hurricane strength winds are possible in the area within the next 48 hours (2 days). This time is based on the eye of the storm, not the outer bands. You can expect to feel the rain and winds before the eye arrives.

A **hurricane warning** means that hurricane strength winds are expected in the area within the next 36 hours (1 1/2 days).

Your parents will be packing a "disaster bag." You should pack a bag of toys, books, cards, and games that will keep you busy if there is no electricity. Gather a flashlight, some of your favorite clothes, shoes to wear after the storm (sneakers or other closed-toed shoes), and a pillow and blanket or sleeping bag.

If you live along the coast, you may have to evacuate (leave) your home in order to stay safe. Your parents will decide whether you need to go to a shelter, or you should travel to stay with friends or family who live in a safer area. If you remain in your home, plan to stay in a room without windows (maybe a big closet) during the worst part of the storm.

Your parents will be very busy getting the house ready for the storm. See what you can do to help.

If your windows are boarded up, it will be dark inside the house—even during the day. Don't get scared. Think of it like being in a special fort.

Gather food that doesn't need to be refrigerated and can be eaten without being cooked. Remember to pack a can opener! Fill as many containers with water as possible. That way you will have drinking water after the storm goes by. There should be at least one gallon of drinking water per person per day for a week.

Animal Behavior—Scientific or Observation?

What do animals do during natural disasters? Can animal behavior help us to predict certain natural disasters, such as earthquakes and tsunamis? These are questions that scientists would like to answer.

Scientists who study animal behavior are biologists. We learn a lot about animal behavior from the animals that live in zoos and aquariums. However, to learn more about wild animals, biologists sometimes put monitors or satellite tags on the animals so they can see where they go. In some cases, the animals have been injured or cared for in a wildlife rehabilitation hospital and are tagged before being released. In other cases, biologists go into the field, secure an animal, calm it, give it a physical examination, put the tag on, and then let the animal go. By following animal movements, biologists can get a good feel for how far and when animals travel, which helps us understand them better.

In order to understand animal behavior, biologists use the same scientific methods that you learn about:

- Ask a question, such as "what do wild animals do before or during a hurricane?"
- Do background research, observe
- Construct a hypothesis
- Test the hypothesis to make sure the results are repeatable and verifiable
- Collect and analyze data
- Draw a conclusion
- Communicate the results

The animal behaviors mentioned in the story are based on various observations. Some of the behaviors were documented by biologists and others were not. Can you figure out which behaviors are just observations and which have some scientific proof? If you were a biologist, what would be your hypothesis about each animal's behavior? How could you test your hypothesis? Who knows, when you grow up, maybe you will be the biologist who can prove it!

Fishermen say that fishing is usually good right before a hurricane because the fish are really biting. They believe the fish are eating as much as possible before the storm stirs up the water, making it more difficult to find food. After Hurricane Charley hit Florida, scientists who had been monitoring fish sounds noted that the fish were louder during the storm and for three days after.

During the hurricane season of 2004, Harbor Branch Oceanographic Institute researchers observed that dolphins living in the Indian River stayed in deep water pockets in their home territory. The researchers also observed lagoon-living dolphins in the Florida Keys seeking deeper, calmer water, staying under water for as long as possible to avoid the wind and waves.

Scientists from the USGS Sirenia Project used to think that manatees swam up river basins to wait out hurricanes. But manatee monitoring during Hurricanes Katrina (as it crossed Florida) and Wilma showed that they stayed offshore where food was plentiful and they could hunker down. Manatees can stay underwater for up to 15 to 20 minutes before coming up for air.

Birders and ornithologists (bird scientists) have observed that some birds delay migration until after hurricanes have passed. They believe that the birds can detect the changes in the air pressure. The scientists have also found seabirds that the winds carried and left hundreds of miles from the area they normally live.

All of the endangered American crocodiles survived Hurricane Andrew. Scientists don't know where they went during the storm.

Scientists from Mote Marine Laboratory's Center for Shark Research have documented tagged sharks heading to deeper water before Tropical Storm Gabrielle and Hurricanes Gordon and Charley arrived. They believe the sharks sense the falling pressure of an approaching storm through their inner ears.

Scientists studying lobster movements and migrations observe that lobsters tend to move to deeper water areas before and during a storm. They believe that the deeper water is not only calmer and colder but that the saltwater is less affected by the rain.

Butterflies in a rainforest exhibit at the Florida Museum of Natural History hid in tree hollows and under rocks a few hours before the arrival of Hurricane Jeanne.

Rabbits and other small animals seem to take cover in underground burrows, hopefully above where the storm surge will hit.

To my grandchildren, Jaxon, Libby, Jillian, Wilson, and Macy: a constant source of joy and inspiration—PZ

Thanks to Erica Rule, Outreach Coordinator, and Neal Dorst, Research Meteorologist, both of NOAA's Atlantic Oceanographic and Meteorological Laboratory, for verifying the hurricane information and to the many scientists and researchers who verified the animal information:

Fish: James Locascio, Graduate Student and Dr. David Mann, Assistant Professor, Biological Oceanography at the University of South Florida College of Marine Science

Dolphins: Stephen D. McCulloch, Founder/Program Manager, Marine Mammal Research and Conservation Program Center for Marine Ecosystems Health Harbor Branch Oceanographic Institute at Florida Atlantic University

Sharks: Dr. Michelle Heupel, Research Director, Australian Institute of Marine Science, James Cook University and Tim Oldread, Director, Center for School and Public Programs, Mote Marine Laboratory

Lobsters: Dr. William H. Howell, Professor of Zoology, University of New Hampshire, Zoology Department

Manatees: Catherine A. Langtimm, Wildlife Biologist, USGS, Sirenia Project

Birds: Dr. Douglas Levey, Professor of Zoology, University of Florida

Crocodiles: Dr. Frank Mazzotti, Wildlife Biologist, University of Florida

Butterflies: Dr. Thomas C. Emmel, Professor of Entomology and Director of the McGuire Center for Lepidoptera and Biodiversity at the University of Florida

Publisher's Cataloging-In-Publication Data

Zelch, Patti R.   Ready, set ... WAIT! : what animals do before a hurricane / by Patti R. Zelch ; illustrated by Connie McLennan.

p. : col. ill. ; cm.

Summary: A hurricane is forming over the ocean. Humans get ready by boarding up windows and gathering food and supplies. But what do wild animals do before and during hurricanes? Based on scientific research and noted observations, this book answers that question about a variety of different animals. Includes "For Creative Minds" educational section.

ISBN: 978-1-60718-072-2 (hardcover)
ISBN: 978-1-60718-083-8 (paperback)
Also available as eBooks featuring auto-flip, auto-read, 3D-page-curling, and selectable English and Spanish text and audio
Interest level: 004-009
Grade level: P-4
ATOS™ Level: 3.0
Lexile Level: 710 Lexile Code: AD

1. Animal behavior--Juvenile literature. 2. Instinct--Juvenile literature. 3. Survival--Juvenile literature. 4. Hurricanes--Juvenile literature. 5. Animals--Habits and behavior. 6. Hurricanes. I. McLennan, Connie. II. Title.

QL751.5 .R4 2010
591.512   2010921904

Manufactured in China, June, 2010
This product conforms to CPSIA 2008
First Printing

Sylvan Dell Publishing
976 Houston Northcutt Blvd., Suite 3
Mt. Pleasant, SC 29464